Down the Rabbit Holes of Wisdom

Discovering Knowledge, Understanding, and God's Guidance in Everyday Life

Rene' Stanley

Books by Rene'

ISBN: 979-8-9997823-9-7 (paperback)

Library of Congress Control Number: 2026910504

Book Cover by: Rene' Stanley

Contents

Introduction

How a Hobby Became a Journey

It all started with a simple coloring book.

I wasn't trying to become an artist. I wasn't thinking about selling anything, learning new software, or building a brand. I just wanted something quiet and calming to do at the end of a long day. A stack of adult coloring books, a handful of pencils and markers, and a little bit of silence—that was enough for me.

But then my curiosity woke up.

I began to wonder why some colors blended more smoothly than others. I noticed how certain pages buckled under wet markers while others held up just fine. I found myself asking questions: *What are the best colored pencils? Does the paper quality really matter this much? Are wax pencils better than chalk pastels? What about markers and gel pens?*

Those questions led me to a place many of us know very well: what I like to call **YouTube University**. One video turned into a playlist, and one playlist turned into late nights watching artists explain shading, blending, paper weights, color theory, and tools I had never even heard of. A quiet little hobby began to pull me down a rabbit hole of learning.

And I didn't stop at coloring books.

Before long, I went from filling in someone else's designs to using AI to create my own digital images. The same curiosity that made me want better pencils made me want to know what else was possible. So I learned how to generate art, tweak it, refine it—over and over again. Eventually, I looked up and realized I had created *thousands* of images.

That raised a new question: *What am I going to do with all of these?*

That one question led me down another rabbit hole. I started turning my images into note cards and greeting cards. From there, it spread to coffee mugs, t-shirts, and anything else I could reasonably press, print, or customize from home. I learned how to use Canva and other design apps to make my ideas look more polished. I kept following the next curiosity, the next "what if," the next little nudge.

Then I discovered that I could upload some of my art as stock images. That meant learning how those platforms work, what kinds of images they accept, what people search for, and how to present my work so it could actually be found. One rabbit hole at a time, my simple coloring hobby began to reshape how I saw creativity, possibility, and even myself.

These creative rabbit holes started about seven years ago.

But in the last two years, something new emerged.

One day, a Reverend from my church was sharing what she was going through trying to get her book published. As I listened, something lit up inside me—the same spark that had once made me search for the perfect pencil or the right kind of paper. I didn't just hear her struggle; I heard an invitation. It was as if God whispered, *Pay attention. There's something here for you, too.*

That moment became another rabbit hole.

I began to explore the world of writing and publishing. Not just the idea of writing, but everything that comes with it: getting the words out of my head and onto the page, editing them, formatting them, designing covers, and figuring out how to actually get a finished book into the hands of readers. I learned about self-publishing, ISBNs, print-on-demand, trim sizes, and more terms than I ever expected to care about.

And just like with coloring and art, one step led to another.

What started as curiosity became a calling. Over time, I wrote **over 30 books**. Many of the ideas for those books didn't come from long planning sessions or complicated strategies. They came from something simple—a single word, a phrase from a sermon, a line spoken in a church service that stayed in my spirit. God often used one small sentence to open up an entire book's worth of thought.

If you look back over your own life, have you noticed that pattern too? How one small interest, one conversation, one offhand comment can send you in a completely new direction?
How a "just for fun" activity can turn into a deep well of learning and growth?

That's what happened to me.

One early morning, before God turned the lights on outside, I found myself awake in that quiet space where the world is still and thoughts can rise to the surface. In that silence, a question came:

What comes first—knowledge, understanding, or wisdom?

I didn't brush it off. I sat with it.

I thought about all the rabbit holes I had gone down—coloring, tools, AI, stock images, design software, self‑publishing, and writing book after book. Each area started with something I *didn't* know. I had to look it up, try it out, experiment, and fail a few times. I gained *knowledge* as I learned. Over time, that knowledge started to make more sense—I began to see patterns and connections. That's where *understanding* grew. And then, little by little, I began to make better choices about what to create, what to focus on, and how to spend my time. That's when it started to look like *wisdom*.

Knowledge, understanding, wisdom.
It sounded simple at first, but the more I thought about it, the deeper it went.

I realized that this wasn't just true for hobbies and creative work. It was true for walking with God. We can know Bible verses. We can understand doctrines and teachings. But at some point, what we know and understand has to turn into how we live, how we love, how we forgive, how we make decisions, and how we respond when life doesn't go the way we hoped.

That's wisdom.

So I found myself asking more questions:

- When it comes to God, what does it really mean to have *knowledge*?

- How does *understanding* grow from that knowledge?

- And what does *wisdom* look like in everyday life—not just in big, dramatic moments, but in the quiet choices we make every day?

Maybe you've wondered about those things too, even if you didn't use those exact words. Maybe you've read the Bible and thought, *I know what it says, but I'm not sure I really understand it.* Or maybe you've understood it clearly, but struggled with what to do next. How do you move from reading Scripture to actually living it in a way that draws you closer to God?

This book was born out of that early-morning question.
It was born out of rabbit holes and curiosity, out of sermons and phrases that wouldn't leave me alone, out of art supplies and AI tools, out of note cards and coffee mugs and over 30 books. But more than anything, it was born out of a desire to walk more closely with God—to not just know *about* Him, but to know Him, understand His ways more deeply, and live wisely in response.

As you read these pages, I don't want you to feel like you're sitting in a classroom taking notes. I want you to feel like we're sitting across from each other, just talking—about life, about faith, about the Bible, and about the ways God meets us in both the ordinary and the unexpected. I'll share some of my journey, and I'll invite you to think about yours.

So before we go any further, let me ask you:

- What rabbit holes has God used in your life to teach you something?

- Where have your questions led you somewhere deeper than you expected?

- And when you think about knowledge, understanding, and

wisdom, which one do you feel most hungry for right now?

Wherever you are, you're welcome here.
This is not a "step‑by‑step" manual or a checklist. It's a conversation and a journey—one that starts with a simple question in the dark before dawn and follows it toward the light of God's Word.

In the chapters ahead, we'll explore what the Bible (*The Record*) says about knowledge, understanding, and wisdom, and how they fit together. We'll talk about how we approach Scripture, how the LORD helps us see what we might have missed, and how all of this begins to shape the way we live each day.

My hope is that, as you walk through these pages, you'll find yourself not only learning *about* these three words, but recognizing them in your own story—and seeing how God has been gently leading you down His own rabbit holes of wisdom all along.

When you're ready, let's step into the first part of that journey together:

Where wisdom really begins.

Part I

The Foundation: Wisdom, Understanding, and Knowledge

Books by Rene'

Chapter 1

The Fear of the Lord

Where Wisdom Really Begins

When we hear the word *wisdom*, a lot of different pictures might come to mind.

Maybe you think of someone older, with gray hair and a calm voice. Maybe you picture a person who always seems to "just know" what to say, or who never seems rattled when life goes sideways. Or maybe, if you're honest, wisdom feels like one of those church words that everyone nods at, but not many people stop to really think about.

The Bible gives us a surprising starting point. It doesn't say, "The beginning of wisdom is reading a lot of books," or "The beginning of wisdom is being very smart." Instead, it says:

> *"The fear of the Lord is the beginning of wisdom,*
> *and the knowledge of the Holy One is understanding."*
> **— Proverbs 9:10 (KJV)**

That phrase can sound a little unsettling at first.
Fear of the Lord.
What does that even mean?

For some people, the word *fear* brings back memories of being yelled at, punished, or controlled. Others might think of fear as wanting to run away and hide. So when we read that wisdom begins with "the fear of the Lord," it's easy to misunderstand it and imagine God as someone we should be terrified of, always waiting to catch us doing something wrong.

But that's not the kind of fear the Bible is talking about.

The "fear of the Lord" is more like the feeling you get when you stand at the edge of the ocean and realize how small you are compared to the waves. It's what happens inside you when you look up at a night sky full of stars and something in you whispers, *There is no way this is an accident.* It's a deep awareness that God is holy, powerful, wise, and good—and that we are not in charge.

It's not the fear that makes you run away; it's the kind of reverence that makes you lean in.

Have you ever had a moment where you suddenly became aware that God was closer than you realized?
Maybe it was during a song in church, or a sermon that felt like it had your name written on it. Maybe it was in a hospital room, a quiet car ride, or in the middle of a situation where you had no idea what to do. In that moment, did you feel something in your heart shift—like you needed to sit up straighter on the inside?

That feeling is part of what it means to fear the Lord.

Wisdom doesn't begin when we say, "I have it all figured out."
Wisdom begins when we say, "God, *You* know more than I do."

It's the place where we stop treating God like a distant symbol in our lives and start recognizing Him as the center. It's when we move from using God like an emergency button to honoring Him as the One who already knows the end from the beginning.

When I think about the fear of the Lord, I think about all the times I tried to handle things on my own first.

I can't count how many times I have gone down a new rabbit hole—whether it was art supplies, software, or publishing tools—determined to figure it out myself. I'd watch videos, test things out, open ten tabs on my browser, and push myself to understand everything as fast as possible. That kind of drive can be helpful in some areas, but spiritually, it can be a problem.

Many of us can be tempted to approach God the way we approach something new we're trying to figure out:

If I do this, maybe I'll get that result. We may not say it out loud, but sometimes we can slip into treating prayer like a button we press when we want something to change.

But God is not a tool, a method, or a system for us to manage. He is the Lord.

And wisdom begins when we remember who He is—and who we are in relation to Him.

Have you ever caught yourself trying to manage God—trying to fit Him into your plans, your timing, your expectations?
Maybe you've felt frustrated when He didn't answer as quickly as you wanted, or in the way you expected. Maybe you've tried to "figure Him

out" instead of bowing your heart and saying, "Lord, I don't understand everything, but I trust You."

That's where the fear of the Lord comes in. It's the recognition that God is worthy of our trust even when we don't have all the answers. It's saying, "You are God. I am not. Please teach me."

Proverbs 9:10 ties wisdom to this posture of reverence: *"The fear of the Lord is the beginning of wisdom, and the knowledge of the Holy One is understanding."* Wisdom doesn't start with the *what* of life—what to do, what to say, what decision to make. Wisdom starts with the *Who*.

Before we ever ask, "What should I do?" the deeper question is, "Who am I listening to?" If God is just one opinion among many, wisdom will always feel slippery. But if He is the *ADONAI* (Lord)—the One whose voice carries the most weight—then we have a firm place to start.

Think about the people in your life whose opinions really matter to you.
There might be many people you casually listen to, but only a few whose words can actually change your mind or calm your heart. Why is that? Usually, it's because you trust their character. You know something about who they are.

Wisdom with God works the same way. The more we recognize who He is—holy, loving, just, merciful, patient, and powerful—the more we take Him seriously. And the more we take Him seriously, the more His Word starts to shape how we think.

Maybe you've noticed this in your own life already.
Perhaps there was a time when a verse you had heard for years suddenly began to carry more weight. It didn't change on the page, but

something changed in you. You weren't just reading words—you were hearing the voice of Someone you knew deserved your full attention.

That's the fear of the Lord at work.

It's not about walking around scared that God is waiting to punish you.
It's about walking through life aware that God is present, God is holy, and God is worthy of your deepest respect and obedience.

Have you ever noticed that when you respect someone, you listen differently?
You slow down. You lean in. You don't brush off what they say. Sometimes you even change your plans because of their perspective. Now imagine living that way with God—not out of terror, but out of deep honor. That's where wisdom begins.

If we try to start with knowledge alone—collecting Bible facts, Christian quotes, and bits of information—we might become informed, but not necessarily wise. If we try to jump straight to wisdom—wanting good outcomes, good decisions, and good reputations—without first honoring God, we end up chasing results without relationship.

The fear of the Lord brings our hearts into the right posture.
It says, "Lord, I want to see life the way You see it. I want to learn from You, not just ask You to approve what I've already decided."

As you think about your own journey, you might want to pause and ask yourself:

When I make decisions, whose voice do I value most? Do I find myself treating God more like a helper or like the Lord of my life? What would it look like, in this season, to live with a deeper awareness of His presence and His holiness?

You don't have to have perfect answers.
This isn't about pretending to be more spiritual than you feel. It's about being honest with God and letting that honesty be the starting place.

The beautiful thing is that God doesn't ask us to clean ourselves up before we come to Him. He invites us to come honestly, to recognize who He is, and to let that recognition shape us. The fear of the Lord doesn't push us away from Him; it draws us closer, with a humble heart that says, "Teach me. Lead me. Show me."

Proverbs 9:10 reminds us that wisdom and understanding are both rooted in relationship: the fear of the Lord, and the knowledge of the Holy One. Before we talk about knowledge, understanding, and wisdom as separate ideas, we have to see that they are all anchored in *who God is.*

In the chapters ahead, we'll talk more about knowledge, understanding, and wisdom. But this is where we have to begin: with the One who gives all three. Before we explore what we can learn, we honor the God who teaches. Before we ask for understanding, we bow before the One whose thoughts are higher than ours. Before we seek wisdom for our lives, we remember that our lives belong to Him.

Wisdom's first step is not a strategy, a system, or a study plan.
Wisdom's first step is worship.

And as we stand there—heart bowed, eyes lifted—we begin to see that this journey into knowledge, understanding, and wisdom is really a journey into the heart of God Himself.

In the next chapter, we'll start with that first word: **knowledge**. What does it really mean to know God's truth—and how does that differ from simply collecting information? Let's go there together.

14

Chapter 2

Knowledge

The Starting Place

If wisdom is about walking with God in a way that shapes our choices and our lives, then knowledge is often where that walk begins.

When we hear the word *knowledge*, we might picture textbooks, degrees, or someone who always seems to have the right answer on the tip of their tongue. In our everyday world, knowledge is often measured by how much information a person can hold, recall, or explain.

But in the Bible, knowledge is more than information.
It has to do with truth, yes—but also with relationship.

Proverbs 9:10, the same verse that tells us *"The fear of the Lord is the beginning of wisdom,"* goes on to say, *"and the knowledge of the Lord is understanding."* Knowledge here is not just about knowing facts *about* God; it's about knowing *God Himself*—the "Lord."

That's an important difference.

You can know a lot *about* a person you've never met. You can read their biography, follow their posts, listen to their interviews, and still not have a real relationship with them. But when you know someone personally—when you've walked with them, talked with them, and shared your heart with them—that knowledge feels different. It's deeper. It's alive.

The same is true with God.

There's a kind of knowledge that simply collects Bible facts, dates, names, and verses. And there's a kind of knowledge that grows as we encounter God in His Word, in prayer, in worship, and in the everyday ups and downs of life. That second kind of knowledge changes us.

Have you ever noticed that the more time you spend with someone, the more you begin to recognize their voice—sometimes even without seeing their face? You might hear them in another room and know immediately who it is. That's what real knowledge does: it makes recognition possible.

In a similar way, as we grow in the knowledge of God, we begin to recognize His voice, His character, and His ways more clearly. We start to sense when something lines up with who He is—and when it doesn't. This is why knowledge is such an important starting place: it introduces us to the God who is inviting us to walk with Him.

But let's be honest: gaining knowledge about God often feels less dramatic than we expect.

Often it looks like slow, steady exposure to His Word. Reading a passage and not understanding all of it at once. Hearing a sermon that plants a seed we don't fully see until years later. Having a verse stick with us for reasons we can't explain. Little by little, something is being built.

Think about your own life for a moment.
What were some of the first things you learned about God?

Maybe it was that He is love. Maybe it was that He is holy. Maybe it was that Jesus died and rose again. Whatever those early truths were, they were the beginning of knowledge. They were the first building blocks on which more would be added.

Just like with my creative journey, knowledge often starts with a simple question: *What is this? How does this work? Who is behind all of this?* When I first started watching videos and reading about art supplies and tools, I wasn't an expert. I was just curious. But that curiosity brought me into contact with information that changed what I could see and do.

In a similar way, spiritual knowledge often begins with a nudge of curiosity.
What does this verse mean?
Why did Jesus say that?
What is God really like?

Sometimes we feel guilty for having questions, as if a strong believer should never wonder or wrestle. But questions, when brought to God, can be the doorway to deeper knowledge. They show that we care enough to seek.

Have you ever felt a little embarrassed about not knowing as much Bible as you think you "should"?
Maybe you've been around people who can quote chapter and verse for almost everything, and you've thought, *I could never be like that.* If that's you, I want you to hear this clearly: God is not shaming you for what you don't know. He's inviting you into what you *can* know—starting right where you are.

You can name it directly like this in your draft:

There's a verse in the New Testament where the apostle Paul prays that believers would be *"ask God to fill you with the knowledge of His will in all the wisdom and understanding which the Spirit gives."* That prayer tells us something important: knowledge is not just a human effort. God Himself wants to fill us with the knowledge of His will. He wants us to know Him. This prayer comes from Colossians 1:9 (CJB).

That means you don't have to force your way into knowledge.
You can ask for it.

You can say, "Lord, I want to know You better. I want to understand Your Word. I want to recognize Your voice in my life." That kind of prayer is not annoying to God. It delights Him.

But while knowledge is a gift, it still grows through exposure.

Imagine someone who buys the best art supplies money can buy—expensive pencils, markers, paints, brushes, paper—but never opens the packages. They have everything they need to create something beautiful, but they don't gain any knowledge of how those tools work because they never use them.

In the same way, we can have access to Bibles, sermons, teachers, and resources, but if we never draw near, never open, never listen, our knowledge will remain thin. It's not about earning God's favor; it's about opening the door to hear what He's already saying.

Maybe you've had seasons where you read the Bible more regularly, and others where it sat unopened. Maybe you've gone stretches where you felt hungry to learn, and other stretches where you felt numb or distracted. Most of us have experienced that up-and-down pattern.

What's important is not that you've been perfectly consistent, but that you're still willing to come back.

Knowledge grows when we keep returning to God—again and again, with open hearts.

Think about how you learn any new subject. At first, the words and concepts feel heavy and unclear. Over time, the language becomes more familiar. You start to notice patterns. You begin to see how pieces fit together. That's knowledge settling in.

When we read Scripture, we may not grasp everything we read, but something is being planted. Stories, parables, psalms, and promises begin to form a framework in our minds. Even if we can't quote them exactly, they become reference points in our hearts.

Have you ever been in a situation where a verse or a truth you didn't even realize you remembered suddenly came back to you at just the right time? Maybe you were struggling with fear, and a verse about God's peace came to mind. Or you were wrestling with shame, and a reminder of His forgiveness surfaced.

That's knowledge bearing fruit.

But there is also a caution here. Knowledge, by itself, can become dangerous if it's not joined to humility and love. It's possible to know a lot about the Bible and still be harsh, proud, or unkind. It's possible to win arguments and lose hearts. That's not the kind of knowledge this book is pointing us toward.

The knowledge that draws us closer to God doesn't puff us up; it opens us up.

It doesn't make us look down on others; it helps us see our own need more clearly.

It doesn't just sharpen our minds; it softens our hearts.

So as we think about knowledge as the starting place, here are a few gentle questions for you to consider:

- When you think of "knowing God," what comes to your mind first—facts, feelings, experiences, or something else?

- Have there been moments when something you learned about God changed the way you saw yourself or your situation?

- Is there an area right now where you feel a fresh curiosity to know God better?

You don't have to force your way into becoming a "Bible expert." That's not the goal. The goal is to grow in the knowledge of the Holy One—to become more familiar with who God is, what He says, and how He moves.

As we keep walking, that knowledge will begin to connect in deeper ways.

That's where the next word comes in: *understanding*.

Knowledge is like gathering pieces of a puzzle. Understanding is when you start to see the picture they form.

In the next chapter, we'll talk about that step—how God takes the truths we've gathered and begins to arrange them in a way that brings clarity, comfort, and direction. For now, it's enough to remember this:

- You are not behind.

- You are not disqualified.

- Wherever you are in what you know, God can begin with you there.

And every bit of true knowledge of Him is a step closer to His heart.

Chapter 3

Understanding

Seeing the Connections

Knowledge gathers the pieces.
Understanding begins to see the picture.

By now, you may have noticed a pattern in how God has worked in your life. There are seasons when you seem to be collecting truths—Bible verses, sermons, conversations, life lessons—and then, almost suddenly, some of those pieces begin to connect. It's not that you learned something completely new, but that you saw what you already knew in a new way.

That's the work of understanding.

If knowledge answers the question, *"What is true?"*
understanding starts to answer, *"How does this fit together, and why does it matter?"*

Think about a time when you heard a familiar Scripture, one you thought you already understood, but this time it landed differently. Maybe the words were the same, but your situation had changed. Or your heart was more open. Or the LORD simply shined a light in a new way. Suddenly, that verse wasn't just *true*—it was *personal*.

That shift—that movement from "I know this" to "I see how this speaks into my life right now"—that's understanding.

When the Puzzle Pieces Start to Touch

Understanding is like working on a puzzle. At first, all you have are scattered pieces—colors, shapes, edges. You might find a corner here, a straight edge there, a patch of blue sky or green grass. It's progress, but it doesn't look like much.

Then, one day, you connect a few sections. The sky meets the tree line. The house meets the path. Suddenly, you can see more than lines and colors—you can see a scene beginning to emerge.

Our journey with God often works the same way.

We may learn about God's love in one season, His faithfulness in another, and His forgiveness in yet another. We hear about His holiness, His patience, His justice. We read about His mercy in the Gospels and His power in the Old Testament. All of these truths are pieces.

Understanding is what happens when those pieces start coming together, and we begin to see God's heart more clearly.

Have you ever had a moment where something you went through years ago suddenly made more sense because of something you're walking through now?
Maybe an old struggle now helps you comfort someone else.
Maybe a past disappointment prepared you for a door God just opened.

In that moment, it's as if God whispers, *"See? I was teaching you even then."*
That's understanding.

the LORD and the "Aha" Moments

One of the beautiful things about understanding is that it's not something we create by sheer effort. We can't force it. We can study, read, and reflect (and we should), but there is a part of understanding that only God can give.

Jesus promised that the LORD would teach us and bring things to our remembrance. There are times when a verse comes to mind at just the right moment, or a truth becomes clear in a way it never has before. That is more than mental clarity; it is spiritual light.

You might experience it like this:

- You've read a passage many times. One day, a phrase stands out and won't let you go.

- You're in a situation where you don't know what to say, and suddenly a truth you've learned comes back with fresh strength.

- You're listening to a sermon, and it feels like the message is stitching together several different things God has been showing you over time.

Understanding often arrives as an "aha" moment—but those moments are built on many quiet, faithful moments of listening, reading, and walking with God.

Have you had times when something "clicked" only after you'd heard it multiple times?
It's easy to think, *Why didn't I get this before?*

But maybe it wasn't that you were careless—it may simply be that your heart, circumstances, or maturity are now in a place where you can see what you couldn't see then.

Understanding comes on God's timetable, not ours.

When Life and Scripture Meet

Understanding grows when what we know from Scripture collides with what we live in everyday life.

For example, you might know the verse that says God will never leave you nor forsake you. You may be able to quote it, underline it, put it on a bookmark. That's knowledge.

Then you walk through a season where you feel alone—maybe misunderstood, overlooked, or physically by yourself. In that lonely place, you sense God's presence in a way you never have before. Suddenly, "I will never leave you" isn't just a comforting sentence; it's a lived reality. That's understanding deepening.

Or you might know that God is patient. You've read it, heard it, even said it. Then you go through a season where you keep stumbling in the same area, and each time you come back to God, you find mercy instead of rejection. You begin to see that His patience is not an abstract idea—it's the way He's been dealing with you all along.

Understanding takes what we know and anchors it in real life.

Can you think of a truth about God that you "knew" long before you actually understood it?
Maybe you didn't fully see it until you needed it.
Maybe you believed it in general but only embraced it as personal later.

Those are moments when knowledge begins to take root.

Connecting Truths, Not Just Collecting Them

In earlier seasons of our walk, it can be easy to think the goal is to learn as many spiritual truths as possible. We might even feel pressure to "catch up" to others who seem to know more. But understanding reminds us that this is not a race and that God is not impressed with how many spiritual facts we can recite.

He is after a heart that sees Him more clearly.

Understanding is what helps us connect truths like:

- God's love and God's holiness

- His mercy and His justice

- His forgiveness and His call to repentance

- His sovereignty and our responsibility

At first, these pairs can feel like tensions. How can God be both loving and just? How can He forgive and still call us to change? How is He in control and yet still hold us accountable for our choices?

When understanding grows, we begin to see that these are not contradictions—they are parts of a larger picture of who God is. The more we see that picture, the more we trust Him, even when not everything makes sense.

Have you ever bounced between two truths, feeling like you had to choose one and ignore the other?

Understanding lets us hold more of what God has said together, without losing balance.

Patience with the Process

Understanding often comes slowly, and that can be frustrating.

We want instant clarity:

- "Lord, explain this now."

- "Show me why this happened."

- "Make this Scripture make sense today."

But, just as it takes time for a seed to become a plant, understanding usually unfolds over time. We might not see what God is doing in the middle of a situation. Sometimes, we have to live through something, look back, and only then do we begin to see that God was teaching, guiding, and shaping us.

It can be helpful to remember:

Some understanding comes quickly.

Some understanding comes gradually.

Some understanding may only fully make sense in eternity.

That doesn't mean we stop seeking. It simply means we seek with humility, recognizing that God's wisdom goes far beyond ours.

Is there something in your life right now that you wish you understood better?

A "why" that you keep bringing to God?
It might be that you're in the middle of the story, and the understanding is still being written.

Welcoming Understanding

While understanding is something God gives, we can posture our hearts to receive it.

We do that when we:

- Stay open instead of shutting down when something doesn't make sense.

- Keep coming back to God's Word, even when it feels familiar.

- Bring our questions to God honestly, without pretending we're fine when we're not.

- Pay attention to patterns—how God repeats certain themes in our reading, conversations, or circumstances.

You don't have to be "deep" to receive understanding. You just need to be willing.

Sometimes, understanding comes in the quiet: a verse that settles in your heart, a thought that brings peace, a sense of "Oh—that's what You were doing, Lord." Other times, it comes through people—a wise word, a testimony, a story that makes something finally clear.

Could it be that God has already been giving you glimpses of understanding, and you're just now recognizing them?

From Understanding to Wisdom

If knowledge gathers truth, and understanding sees how that truth fits into our lives, then wisdom is what happens when we start to live in light of that understanding.

- Knowledge says, "God is faithful."

- Understanding says, "I see how God has been faithful to me."

- Wisdom says, "Because God is faithful, I will trust Him in this decision."

Each step builds on the last.

In this chapter, we've been sitting mainly with that middle step: the way God takes us from "I know this" to "I see this" to "I feel this changing how I view everything." That's the quiet work of understanding, and it is just as much a gift from God as anything else.

As you reflect, you might ask yourself:

- What truths about God are beginning to connect for me in this season?

- Where have I started to see meaning in things that once just felt random or painful?

- Are there areas where I sense that understanding is still forming, even if I don't see it clearly yet?

You don't have to rush this process. Understanding is not a test you pass; it's a light God turns on, one room at a time.

In the next chapter, we'll talk about wisdom—how knowledge and understanding move from ideas in our minds to choices in our daily lives. For now, take comfort in this: if you've been gathering pieces, God is more than able to help you see the picture.

He has been working in you, even in the seasons that felt confusing. And little by little, He is teaching you to see.

Chapter 4

Wisdom

Walking It Out

By now, we've talked about *knowledge*—gathering truth—and *understanding*—beginning to see how those truths fit together and speak into our lives. Wisdom is the next step on that path.

Wisdom is where what we know and what we see begin to shape what we *do*.

You could say it this way:

- Knowledge says, "I know what God says."

- Understanding says, "I see how it applies to me."

- Wisdom says, "I'm going to live like it's true."

Wisdom is truth in motion.

More Than Good Advice

In everyday language, we sometimes use "wisdom" to describe good advice or clever sayings. We might call someone wise because they're calm under pressure or because they usually make smart choices. There's some truth in that, but biblical wisdom goes deeper.

In Scripture, wisdom is tied closely to God Himself. It's not just about being clever; it's about living in alignment with God's character and will. Wisdom isn't just knowing the right thing—it's choosing it, even when it's hard, inconvenient, or costly.

Have you ever known the right thing to do, but struggled to actually do it?
Most of us can say yes to that.
That gap between knowing and doing is where wisdom is needed.

Wisdom bridges that gap.

When Knowledge and Understanding Meet Decisions

Think about a simple example.

You might *know* that it's important to forgive. You've heard sermons, read verses, maybe even shared that truth with someone else. That's knowledge.

You might also *understand* why forgiveness matters. You've seen how bitterness eats away at peace. You've heard stories of people who found freedom when they let go. Maybe you've even experienced that freedom yourself once or twice. That's understanding.

Then someone hurts you deeply.
Your feelings are raw. Your mind is busy building a case. You replay what happened. You think about what you could say back, how you could prove your point or protect yourself.

In that moment, wisdom is not just knowing that forgiveness is right, or understanding why it matters. Wisdom is choosing, with God's help, to walk the path of forgiveness in real time—even when your emotions are slow to follow.

It might be a quiet prayer: "Lord, I know what You say. I understand why You say it. Help me to walk it out here."

That prayer—that step—that's wisdom.

Can you think of a time when what you knew lined up with what you understood, and you still had to make a choice about whether to live it out?
Those crossroads are where wisdom grows.

Wisdom in the Everyday, Not Just the Big Moments

Sometimes we think of wisdom only in terms of big, life-changing decisions—choosing a job, moving to a new place, entering a relationship, starting a ministry. Those moments are important, and we definitely need wisdom in them.

But most of the time, wisdom shows up in the ordinary.

Wisdom is in how we respond when someone speaks to us sharply.
It's in how we handle money when no one is watching.
It's in whether we listen or interrupt.
It's in how we spend our free time, what we feed our minds, and where we let our thoughts wander.

Everyday life is full of small choices that slowly shape who we become.

Have you noticed that some of your biggest regrets came from small decisions that didn't seem like a big deal at the time?

In the same way, some of your greatest blessings may have grown from simple, quiet choices to do what you sensed God leading you to do, even when no one else was clapping for you.

Wisdom lives in those small moments.

Asking for Wisdom

One of the most encouraging things about wisdom is that God doesn't expect us to manufacture it on our own. The Bible tells us that if anyone lacks wisdom, they should ask God, who gives generously and without finding fault.

That means:

- God knows we often don't know what to do.

- He's not annoyed when we admit it.

- He's willing to give wisdom as we seek Him.

Have you ever been in a situation where you whispered, "Lord, I don't know what to say," or "I don't know what to do next," and somehow you had a sense of peace, a phrase to speak, or a quiet nudge about what step to take?

That's often how wisdom comes—not always with a loud announcement, but with a gentle clarity in the middle of confusion.

Wisdom doesn't always mean having all the details.
Sometimes it's just the next right step.

When Wisdom Looks Different Than We Expect

The path of wisdom is not always the path that looks impressive.

- Sometimes, wisdom looks like staying quiet when everything in you wants to prove a point.

- Sometimes, it looks like saying "no" to something that everyone else thinks is an opportunity.

- Sometimes, it looks like apologizing first, even when you feel you were more right than wrong.

- Sometimes, it means waiting when you'd rather rush, or acting when you'd rather stall.

Wisdom often cuts against our natural instincts.

Have you had times when everything in you wanted to react one way, but you sensed God nudging you in a different direction?
Maybe wisdom looked weaker in that moment—but later, you saw that it protected your heart, your relationships, or your testimony.

Wisdom doesn't always make us look strong, but it does keep us anchored in God.

The Fruit of Wisdom

Over time, wisdom begins to leave a trail.

People who walk in wisdom may not have perfect lives, but there are signs:

- They tend to have steadier hearts in storms.

- They are often slower to speak and quicker to listen.

- Their decisions reflect a long‑term view, not just short‑term feelings.

- They carry a quiet peace that doesn't depend on everything going their way.

This doesn't mean they never struggle, never cry, or never make mistakes. Wisdom doesn't erase our humanity. But it does shape how we respond and recover.

If you think about someone you consider wise, what is it that stands out to you?

- Is it their words?

- Their calm?

- Their consistency?

Often, what we're seeing is a life where knowledge, understanding, and obedience have been woven together over time.

Wisdom Is Learned Along the Way

It's important to remember: wisdom grows. It's not something we either have or don't have. It develops as we walk with God.

We learn wisdom when:

- We follow God's leading and see good fruit over time.

- We ignore His leading, experience the consequences, and learn to listen more carefully next time.

- We watch the examples of others—both those who walk wisely and those who don't.

- We reflect on our days and notice where we followed God's nudge and where we resisted it.

Have you ever looked back at a past season and thought, *If I knew then what I know now, I would have chosen differently?*
That's a sign that wisdom has grown in you.

Instead of using that realization to beat yourself up, you can use it to thank God for how far He's brought you—and to walk more wisely in the present.

Walking, Not Sprinting

Wisdom is less like a sprint and more like a walk.

It's built step by step:

- One honest prayer at a time.

- One obedient choice at a time.

- One quiet surrender at a time.

There will be days when you feel wise, and days when you feel like you're stumbling. There will be moments when you clearly sense God's leading, and others when you're just doing the best you can with what you know.

The important thing is not that you get everything right, but that you keep walking with God.

As you think about wisdom in this season of your life, you might ask:

- Is there an area where I've been knowing and understanding, but hesitating to *do*?

- What is one small step of wisdom I sense God inviting me to take right now?

- How can I make a habit of pausing and asking God for wisdom in my everyday decisions?

You don't have to become a "wise person" overnight.
You simply walk with the One who *is* wisdom, and let Him lead you, one step at a time.

As we continue this journey, we'll shift from focusing on these three words in general—knowledge, understanding, and wisdom—to looking at how they show up specifically in how we approach the Bible and how we live our daily lives.

For now, remember this:

- Knowledge helps you see what is true.

- Understanding helps you see how it fits together.

- Wisdom helps you live it out.

And in every part of that journey, God is with you—teaching, guiding, correcting, and encouraging you as you learn to walk with Him.

Part II

Studying the Word of God

Books by Rene'

Studying the Word of God

We've walked through knowledge, understanding, and wisdom as ideas, and as experiences. Now we're going to bring those three words right into the heart of our everyday walk with God—into how we approach the Bible.

For many of us, the Bible has been near us for years—a book on a shelf, on a phone, on a pew in church. Some of us grew up hearing it read out loud. Others came to it later in life. Some have read it cover to cover; others have tried and gotten stuck in the same place more than once.

No matter where you fall on that spectrum, one thing is true: the Bible is not just a book to get through—it is a place to meet God.

God has chosen to reveal Himself through His Word. The stories, poems, letters, and teachings that fill its pages are not just ancient writings; they are living words that God still uses to speak today. But like any deep conversation, it takes time, attention, and a willing heart to listen.

You don't need a seminary degree to read the Bible.
You don't need to know Greek and Hebrew.
You don't even need to have "done it right" in the past.

What you need is a desire to know God—and a willingness to let Him teach you.

In this part of the book, we're going to talk about what it looks like to "go down the rabbit holes" of Scripture. Not in a way that gets lost in arguments or complexity, but in a way that draws you closer to the heart of God. We'll talk about how learning works, how the LORD helps us, how tools can support us, and how steady time in God's Word quietly shapes who we are.

This isn't a reading plan or a list of rules.
It's a conversation about how we *approach* the Word of God.

Let's start with something simple and honest:
how we learn.

Chapter 5

Learning How to Learn

If you've ever picked up a new skill, you already know something about learning—even if you've never put it into a lesson plan.

Remember "YouTube University"?
When I started trying to understand pencils, paper, markers, and later, digital tools, I didn't have a teacher standing over my shoulder. I had curiosity, a screen, and a lot of trial and error.

I watched other people work.
I listened to the way they described what they were doing.
I tried things, messed them up, and tried again.

Slowly, I began to recognize patterns. I learned what to look for, what to avoid, what made things easier, and what made them harder. I began to learn *how* to learn in that area.

Studying the Bible has some similarities—and some big differences.

On the one hand, we still learn through exposure, repetition, and paying attention. We still grow by asking questions and staying curious. On the other hand, we're not just learning a skill; we're learning a Person. We're not just gaining information; we're entering into a relationship with the living God.

That changes everything.

Not a Race, Not a Test

Many people carry quiet pressure when it comes to the Bible.

I should know more by now.

I've been in church for years; I shouldn't be confused.

Everyone else seems to get it faster than I do.

Have any of those thoughts ever passed through your mind?

If they have, let me say this clearly: the Bible is not a race you're losing or a test you're failing. It is God's invitation to hear His heart, in His time, in your real life.

Some seasons of life will allow long, slow mornings with the Word. Others may be full of responsibilities, interruptions, and fatigue. God knows which season you're in. He's not surprised by your life.

The important thing is not how much you read in one sitting, but whether you are willing to come, listen, and keep coming back.

What would change in your heart if you stopped treating Bible reading like an obligation and began to see it as a conversation?
Not, *"I have to get through this chapter,"* but, *"Lord, what would You like to show me today?"*

Curiosity and Reverence Together

When we come to Scripture, we need two things that might seem opposite at first: curiosity and reverence.

Curiosity asks:

- *What does this mean?*

- *Why did Jesus say it that way?*

- *Who was this written to?*

- *How does this connect with what I've read elsewhere?*

Reverence remembers:

- *This is God's Word, not just any book.*

- *These are not just stories; they reveal God's heart and ways.*

- *I'm not here to judge God's Word—I'm here to let it speak into my life.*

When curiosity and reverence are together, something beautiful happens. We're free to ask honest questions, to admit confusion, and to wrestle with difficult passages—but we do so from a place of trust, not suspicion.

Have you ever felt guilty for having questions about the Bible?
As if asking "why" or "how" made you less spiritual?
If so, let's release that pressure.

God is not threatened by your questions.
He already knows you have them.

The key is where you bring them—to your own assumptions, or to Him.

Learning in Layers

Sometimes we expect to understand everything we read right away. When we don't, we're tempted to think, *This just isn't for me,* and close the book.

But the truth is, we often learn in layers.

You might read a passage today and only catch one simple idea. Months or years later, you might read that same passage and notice something you completely missed before. The words didn't change—but *you* did. Your experiences, your questions, and your sensitivity to God's voice all grew.

The Bible is deep enough to speak to you in every season.

Think of it like this: you don't have to drain the whole ocean to benefit from the water. You can stand at the shore, wade in, and still be refreshed. You can learn real, life-changing truth even while much remains beyond your understanding.

Can you remember a time when a familiar verse took on new meaning because of what you were going through?
That's what learning in layers looks like.

Giving Yourself Permission to Be Where You Are

Sometimes, we don't give ourselves permission to be beginners.

If you're new to reading the Bible, it's okay to start simply. The Gospel of John, Psalms, Proverbs—these are often gentle places to begin. If you've known Scripture for years, it's okay to admit there are still parts that confuse you.

You are allowed to be where you are.
You are allowed to grow from there.

Think about your creative rabbit holes. You didn't start by knowing every tool and technique. You started by experimenting. You gave yourself room to learn. What if you extended that same grace to yourself in your walk with God's Word?

What if, instead of saying, *"I should already know this,"* you said, *"Lord, I'm here. Teach me from the beginning if You need to."*

Letting the Bible Read You

One of the mysteries of Scripture is that while we are reading it, it is also "reading" us.

There are moments when a passage exposes our motives, encourages our weary hearts, challenges our behavior, or comforts our fears in a way no ordinary book can. It's as if the words reach inside and put language to what we couldn't quite say.

Have you ever had that happen?
You open your Bible "just to read," and suddenly you feel like God is talking directly to your situation.

That is part of the learning process.
We're not only learning *about* God—we're letting Him show us the truth about ourselves, too.

That can be tender and uncomfortable. But it is also how transformation begins. When we let Scripture do more than inform us—when we let it correct, comfort, and realign us—we're moving from mere knowledge into understanding and stepping toward wisdom.

A Gentle Question for You

As you think about your relationship with the Bible right now, ask yourself:

- Do I see Scripture more as a burden or an invitation?

- Do I approach it with guilt, or with curiosity and reverence?

- What might change if I gave myself permission to learn slowly, layer by layer?

You don't have to have perfect answers.
This is a journey, not a performance.

In the next chapter, we'll talk about someone Jesus promised would walk with us as we read and learn—the Holy Spirit. He is not just the author behind the words; He is the One who helps us understand, remember, and apply them.

You are not reading alone.
Let's talk about the One who reads with you.

Chapter 6

Listening to the Holy Spirit

If you've ever opened your Bible, read a passage, and thought, *I don't get it,* you're not alone.

There are parts of Scripture that are simple and clear, and there are parts that feel deep, layered, and even confusing at first glance. Some verses comfort us right away. Others leave us with questions.

God knew it would be that way.
And He didn't leave us to figure it all out by ourselves.

Jesus made a promise to His followers that still matters for us today:

> "But the Counselor, the Holy Spirit, whom the Father will
> send in my name,
> will teach you everything: that is he will remind you of
> everything I have said to you."
> —John 14:26 (CJB)

the LORD is not just a distant idea or a church phrase. He is a Person—God's presence with us—who teaches, reminds, guides, comforts, and convicts. When it comes to reading and understanding the

Bible, He is our greatest help.

You are not sitting alone with a book.
You are sitting with God, who speaks through His Word by His Spirit.

When Words Come Alive

Have you ever had this experience?

You're reading a familiar passage—something you may have heard since childhood. You've skimmed it before, maybe many times. But one day, a phrase seems to light up on the page. It feels like it's underlined in your heart, even if it isn't on the paper. It meets you exactly where you are.

That's more than a good feeling. That's the LORD at work.

Or maybe this has happened: you're going about your day, not even thinking about Bible reading, and suddenly a verse comes to mind. You didn't plan it. You weren't trying to memorize it. But there it is, right when you need it.

That's the LORD "bringing to remembrance" what you've heard or read.

Sometimes we're tempted to think that those moments are just coincidence. But Jesus said this is part of what the Spirit does—He teaches and reminds.

Have you ever noticed a pattern where the same verse, idea, or story keeps showing up—in sermons, in conversations, in your reading?
It might just be the Spirit highlighting something for you.

The Spirit as Teacher, Not Just Translator

It's easy to think of the LORD only as someone who "translates" Scripture for us—helping us understand the meaning of words. But His role is bigger than that.

He doesn't just explain; He forms.

He uses Scripture to shape our thoughts, soften our hearts, and draw us closer to God. He helps us not only grasp what a passage *says*, but what it is saying to *us* in this moment.

Sometimes that looks like:

- Conviction: a gentle (or strong) awareness that something in our life is out of line with God's heart.

- Comfort: a deep sense of peace or reassurance when we're afraid or discouraged.

- Clarity: a sudden understanding of how a verse applies to a situation we're facing.

- Correction: a redirection in how we're thinking, speaking, or acting.

Have you ever read a verse and felt both "exposed" and loved at the same time?
Like God was telling you the truth about yourself, but not to shame you—to heal you?

That's the Spirit teaching.

Inviting, Not Forcing

The LORD is powerful, but He is also gentle. He doesn't usually shout over the noise of our lives. More often, He nudges.

He might nudge you to:

- Pause on a particular verse instead of rushing past it.

- Go back and read something again.

- Look at a passage from a different angle.

- Pay attention to a word or phrase that stands out.

He doesn't force you to listen, but He invites you.

Have you ever felt a quiet sense of, *"Slow down here—there's something I want you to see,"* while reading Scripture?
Or a feeling that you should go back to a passage you read days ago?

That may well be the Spirit's invitation.

We can respond by simply saying, "Lord, I sense You drawing my attention here. Help me see what You're showing me."

Learning to Recognize His Voice

One of the biggest questions people have is:
How do I know it's the LORD and not just my own thoughts?

That's an honest question. The answer usually isn't a formula; it's a relationship.

Over time, as you walk with God, you begin to recognize the "tone" of His voice—how He speaks through Scripture, how His leadings align with His character, and how His guidance brings peace, even when it's challenging.

Some simple signs that something may truly be from the Holy Spirit:

- It lines up with the overall message and character of Scripture. The Spirit will not contradict the Word He inspired.

- It draws you toward God, not away from Him. Even conviction from the Spirit points you back to God, not into shame that isolates you.

- It produces the kind of fruit Scripture associates with His work—love, joy, peace, patience, kindness, goodness, faithfulness, gentleness, self-control.

- It often comes with a humble clarity, not a prideful rush.

Have you noticed that the Spirit's guidance, even when firm, usually carries a sense of "rightness" and peace underneath it?
Not always comfortable—but steady.

We learn to recognize that over time, just as we learn to recognize a friend's voice after many conversations.

Reading *With* the Spirit

What does it look like, practically, to listen to the LORD as you study the Bible?

It can be as simple and quiet as this:

- Before you read:
  "Holy Spirit, help me understand what I'm about to read. Open my eyes. Show me what I need to see today."

- As you read:
  Pay attention to where you feel drawn, stirred, or unsettled. Notice what comforts you, what challenges you, what raises questions.

- After you read:
  "Is there something from this passage You want me to carry into my day? Is there a step You're inviting me to take, or a truth You want me to hold onto?"

You don't need fancy words.
You just need a willing heart.

Have you ever thought about reading the Bible *with* God, instead of *for* God?
Not trying to impress Him with your consistency, but inviting Him into the moment?

That simple shift can change everything.

When It Feels Quiet

There will be days when you don't feel much of anything.

You read, and the words feel flat.
You pray, and the sky feels quiet.

You look for a nudge, and you're not sure you sense one.

Those days don't mean the Spirit is absent.

Sometimes He is working in ways that are slower, deeper, and less noticeable to us. Just as seeds sprout underground before we see any green, the Word may be taking root in ways we can't yet see. Other times, we might simply be tired, distracted, or in a season where faith means trusting that God is at work even when we don't feel it.

Have you ever looked back on a dry season and realized later that God was still sustaining you through it?
Sometimes we only see the Spirit's work in hindsight.

On those quiet days, it can help to pray, "Lord, I don't feel much right now, but I trust that You are here. Help me stay faithful, even when it feels ordinary."

Trusting the Spirit More Than Your "Performance"

When it comes to reading the Bible, it's easy to judge ourselves by how much we read, how consistently we read, or how many insights we think we gained.

But the deeper question is:

- Am I showing up with an open heart?

- Am I willing to listen, not just finish?

- Am I trusting the LORD to do what Jesus said He would do—teach, remind, and guide?

You don't have to impress God with your reading habits.
You're His child, not His employee.

The Spirit is not grading your performance. He is helping you grow.

A Conversation to Continue

As you think about your own journey, you might pause and consider:

- Have I been trying to understand the Bible only with my own strength?

- What would it look like to invite the LORD into my reading more intentionally?

- Can I remember a time when a verse came alive, or came back to me at just the right moment? How might the Spirit have been at work there?

You don't have to answer all of that at once. Just bring it before God.

Part of listening to the LORD is simply making room—room to be quiet, room to ask, room to notice. He delights in walking with you through Scripture, one passage, one day, one "aha" moment at a time.

In the next chapter, we'll talk about some of the tools that can support us as we study—Bibles, notes, apps, and more—but always with this in mind:

Tools can be helpful.
the LORD is essential.

You are not doing this alone.

Chapter 7

Tools for Deeper Study

By now, you've probably noticed something about how God teaches you:

He meets you where you are, with what you have.

Sometimes that's a quiet moment with just you, a simple Bible, and a soft place to sit. Other times, it might be a sermon, a song, a conversation, or even a video that helps a truth land in a new way. God is not limited in how He reaches us.

In our time, we have access to more tools for studying the Bible than any generation before us—printed Bibles in many translations, study notes, concordances, apps, audio Bibles, videos, reading plans, and more. That can be a blessing...and it can also feel overwhelming.

Have you ever opened a Bible app and felt lost in all the options?
Or picked up a study Bible and wondered, *Where do I even start with all these notes?*

You're not alone.

In this chapter, we're going to talk about tools—but not as a pile of "shoulds." Think of this as a friendly walk through a toolbox, with someone saying, "Here's what this does, here's how it can help, and here's a reminder that you don't need to use everything at once."

You don't need every tool to meet with God.
But some tools can help you pay closer attention to what He's saying.

The Bible Itself: Your First and Primary Tool

It might sound obvious, but it's important to say: the most important "tool" for Bible study is the Bible itself.

Study notes can be helpful. Commentaries can be insightful. Apps can be convenient. But nothing replaces the text of Scripture. That's where God has promised to speak.

Sometimes, the best thing you can do is simply slow down and sit with the words on the page. Read them, read them again, and ask, "Lord, what are You saying here?" Before we reach for other tools, it helps to give the Bible itself our full attention.

Have you ever caught yourself spending more time reading *about* the Bible than actually reading the Bible?
It's an easy trap to fall into.

Other tools are meant to support Scripture, not overshadow it.

Translations: Finding a Voice You Can Hear

One of the blessings we have today is access to multiple Bible translations. Some are more formal and word-for-word, others are more conversational and thought-for-thought. Each has its strengths.

You don't have to pick the "perfect" translation.

You can think in simpler terms: *Can I understand what I'm reading? Does this help me hear the meaning clearly?*

Sometimes, reading a familiar passage in a different translation helps you notice details you've missed before. If one phrasing is hard to grasp, another might open it up.

If you've ever felt stuck, it's okay to compare a few translations side by side and see which one helps the meaning land. That's not being unspiritual—that's paying attention.

Study Bibles and Notes: Helpful, But Not the Final Word

Study Bibles often include notes at the bottom of the page that explain background, clarify difficult phrases, or connect related passages. These can be very helpful, especially when you're curious about context—who wrote this, who they wrote to, and what was happening at the time.

But it's important to remember: notes are written by people.
They are not Scripture themselves.

They can offer insight, but they don't replace listening to God. Sometimes, it's good to read the passage first with no notes, talk to God about it, and then glance at the notes afterward as a way of saying, "Help me see what I might have missed."

Have you ever read a note that helped something finally make sense? Those moments can be like a light turning on. Just keep in mind that the brightest light is still God's Word itself.

Concordances, Cross‑References, and "Following the Threads"

A concordance (or the search feature in a Bible app) can help you find where certain words or themes appear throughout Scripture. Cross-references are those little verse listings in the margin that point you to related passages.

These tools are especially helpful when something catches your attention and you want to see it in a larger context.

For example, if "wisdom" keeps showing up in your reading, you might begin following that word through other books of the Bible. Suddenly, you see that wisdom appears in Proverbs, James, the Gospels, and even in descriptions of Jesus Himself. The more you follow that thread, the richer your understanding becomes.

Have you ever had a theme that seemed to keep popping up everywhere—in verses, sermons, and songs?
Sometimes, tools like concordances and cross-references simply help you see what God is already drawing your attention to.

Journals, Notebooks, and Digital Notes

Writing things down can be a powerful way to notice and remember what God is showing you.

You might:

- Jot down a verse that stood out.

- Write a question you don't have an answer to yet.

- Record a thought like, "This reminds me of what I'm going through at work," or, "I think God is nudging me here."

You don't have to write beautifully or perfectly. This isn't a report; it's a record of a conversation between you and God.

Some people like paper journals. Others prefer note apps, documents, or digital notebooks. The format doesn't matter as much as the heart behind it: *I want to notice what God is saying and make room to come back to it.*

Have you ever gone back to something you wrote months or years ago and realized, *God was preparing me even then?*
That's one of the quiet gifts of keeping notes.

"YouTube University," Podcasts, and Teaching

We live in a time where there is no shortage of Bible teaching available online—videos, podcasts, articles, and more. Some of it is incredibly helpful. It can feel like "YouTube University" for spiritual growth.

Just like with your creative journey, you can learn a lot by watching others who have gone ahead of you—how they study, how they explain, how they apply Scripture.

At the same time, not every voice is equally wise or accurate. That doesn't mean we need to be afraid, but it does mean we should be discerning.

Some simple questions to consider:

- Does this teaching line up with the overall message of Scripture?

- Does it point me toward Jesus, humility, love, and obedience—or toward pride, confusion, and division?

- Does it encourage me to read the Bible for myself, or make me dependent only on the teacher?

Have you ever listened to a message that left you both encouraged and drawn back to the Word itself?
That's a good sign.

Tools that truly help us don't just give us answers—they send us back to Scripture with more hunger.

Bible Apps and Reading Plans

Apps can be a great way to keep Scripture close—especially if you're often on the go. Many offer reading plans, reminders, audio options, and easy ways to highlight or take notes.

A reading plan can give structure when you're not sure where to start. It can help you move through books of the Bible in an intentional way rather than jumping around randomly.

But a plan is a tool, not a master.

If you miss a day (or a week), you are not a failure. If you feel the Spirit drawing you to a different passage than what's on the schedule, it's okay to follow that. The goal is not to finish a plan—it's to keep meeting with God.

Have you ever felt bound by a plan, as if catching up mattered more than connecting with God?
If so, it might be time to loosen the grip a bit.

Let the plan serve the relationship, not replace it.

When Tools Become a Distraction

With so many options, it's possible for tools to distract us from the very God they're supposed to help us see.

We can spend so much time tinkering with highlighters, notes, color-coding, or hunting for the "perfect" resource that we never actually sit quietly with God's Word.

There's nothing wrong with enjoying those things—organization can be a joy. But it's worth asking occasionally:

- Am I using these tools to draw closer to God—or to avoid sitting still with Him?

- Do I feel more excitement about the tools than about the truth they're meant to reveal?

Sometimes, the most powerful thing you can do is put the extras aside and simply say, "Lord, here I am. Speak to me."

Choosing What Helps *You*

Not everyone learns the same way.

Some people absorb Scripture best by reading silently. Others by reading aloud. Some by listening to audio. Some by writing notes. Some by talking it through with others. Many of us need a mix.

You don't have to study the Bible exactly like someone else for it to "count."

God knows how He wired you.

Think back over your life:

- Have there been moments when Scripture felt especially alive to you?

- What were you doing then—reading, listening, discussing, journaling?

- Which tools helped you pay attention, not just pass time?

Those are clues.

You can lean into what helps you truly engage and let go of what feels like pressure without fruit.

A Gentle Invitation

As you consider all these tools—Bibles, notes, apps, journals, videos—remember this:

Tools are servants, not saviors.
They support the conversation; they are not the conversation itself.

The real miracle is that the God of heaven speaks to us at all—and that He invites us to know Him through His Word, by His Spirit, in our everyday lives.

So maybe the question isn't, "Which tools should I be using?"
Maybe it's, "Lord, in this season, what will help me hear You more clearly?"

You might find that in one season, a study Bible is exactly what you need. In another, a simple paperback Bible and a notebook are enough. In another, an audio Bible on your commute becomes your lifeline.

That's okay.
You are allowed to adjust.

In the next chapter, we'll talk about what happens over time as we keep showing up with God's Word—how steady, imperfect, honest time in Scripture slowly shapes the way we think, feel, and live.

For now, take a breath and remember:
You don't have to use every tool.
You just have to be willing to listen.

Chapter 8

Growing Through Study

If you've ever planted something—a flower, a plant, even a tiny herb in a pot—you know this:
growth is usually quiet and slow.

You water. You wait. You check the soil. For a while, nothing seems to change. Then one day, you notice a tiny sprout pushing through the dirt. It didn't appear in that moment—it had been growing the whole time, just out of sight.

Spending time in God's Word often works the same way.

You read, you pray, you listen. Some days a verse jumps off the page. Other days feel ordinary or even dry. But underneath all of that, something is happening. God is using His Word to shape you, even when you don't feel especially "spiritual."

This chapter is about that quiet, steady work—how regular time in Scripture, with the Holy Spirit's help, slowly grows us from the inside out.

Invisible Work

There are seasons when you walk away from reading the Bible feeling encouraged, strengthened, or clearly spoken to. Those moments are beautiful, and we thank God for them.

But there are also days when nothing dramatic happens. You close the Bible and think, *Well, I read. I'm not sure what that did.*

Have you been there?

It's easy in those moments to wonder, *Is this even working?*
But consider this: do you remember every meal you've eaten in your life? Probably not. Yet those meals still nourished you, kept you going, and kept you alive.

In the same way, you may not remember every passage you've read or every insight you've had. But that doesn't mean they didn't do something in you. God often works through repetition and consistency. Truth settles in little by little, almost like layers of paint on a canvas.

What if some of the most "uneventful" days in the Word have actually been some of the most important for your growth?

Renewing the Mind

The Bible talks about our minds being renewed—gradually transformed—so that we begin to see the world more like God sees it.

That doesn't usually happen in one moment. It happens as God's Word slowly pushes back against old patterns of thinking: fear, pride, shame, comparison, hopelessness. Over time, new patterns take their place: trust, humility, grace, gratitude, and hope.

You might notice it in small ways:

- A situation that would've sent you into panic now only stirs concern—and a prayer.

- A comment that would've offended you now rolls off more easily because you know who you are in God.

- A delay that once felt like rejection now feels more like, *"Maybe God is protecting or redirecting me."*

Have you seen any of those shifts in yourself over the years?
They may not have come from a single Bible study moment, but from God's Word working on you over time.

That's growth.

Recognizing God's Voice Sooner

Another sign of growth through study is that you begin to recognize God's voice more quickly.

When you first start learning Scripture, everything might feel new. You're not always sure what's from God, what's from you, and what's from your circumstances. As you spend more time in the Word, you begin to see the patterns of how God speaks, what He values, and what His heart looks like.

Then, when something comes along that doesn't match that, you notice.

- A teaching that twists grace into permission for anything.

- An idea that uses God's name but doesn't reflect His character.

- A thought that sounds "spiritual" but doesn't line up with the truth of Scripture.

Because God's Word has been shaping your spiritual "ear," you're quicker to say, *"Something's not right there."*

Have you ever heard something and felt that check in your spirit, even if you couldn't explain why right away?
That can be the fruit of God's Word forming your discernment over time.

Growing in Patience, Not Just Knowledge

One of the quiet gifts of steady study is patience.

As you read about people in Scripture—Abraham, Moses, David, Esther, Mary, Paul—you begin to see a pattern: God often works over years, not minutes. He makes promises and then allows long stretches of waiting, growth, testing, and preparation.

The more you see that in the Bible, the less strange it feels when God takes His time in your life.

You might still struggle (we all do), but there's a deeper layer underneath that says, *"God has taken His time with others before. Maybe He's doing something I can't see yet."*

Have you noticed that your expectations of God's timing have shifted at all as you've walked with Him?
Maybe not perfectly, but even a little?

That shift is part of maturity. It doesn't come from a single verse—it comes from seeing God's faithfulness woven through Scripture again and again.

From Duty to Desire

For many people, time in God's Word begins as discipline.
You know it's important. You've heard you "should." So you show up, even when it feels more like duty than delight.

There is nothing wrong with that. Discipline is a gift. Sometimes we do what's right long before we feel what's right.

But as you keep returning, something often begins to change. Small moments of connection, understanding, or comfort add up. You start to realize: *I miss this when I skip it.* Not because you're scared of God being mad, but because you're missing a conversation, a grounding, a steadying.

Bit by bit, duty can give birth to desire.

Have you ever noticed that even when you don't "feel like it," you're glad you spent time with God once you do?
That's a sign that your heart is learning where its true food comes from.

Growth Others See Before You Do

Sometimes, other people notice your growth before you do.

You might feel like the same you—still learning, still stumbling, still needing grace. But someone close to you might say:

- "You seem more at peace than you used to be."

- "You don't react the way you once did."

- "You've become more patient, more gentle, more steady."

They're not saying you've become perfect. They're saying they see fruit.

It can be hard to see our own progress because we live inside our thoughts every day. But the people around us often get a clearer view of the before and after.

Have you ever had someone point out growth in you that you hadn't noticed?

Sometimes, that's God's way of saying, *"See? My Word is working."*

Staying Through the Boring and the Hard

Let's be honest: there are parts of the Bible that feel easier to read than others.

Stories about Jesus, psalms of comfort, and encouraging promises often feel very accessible. Genealogies, measurements of the temple, or certain prophetic passages can feel distant or strange.

You don't have to pretend everything is equally easy. But there is value, over a lifetime, in being exposed to the "boring" and the "hard" too. Sometimes, those very places hold treasures that God will unpack for you later.

You might not fully "get" everything in Leviticus, for example, but you might start to sense how serious God is about holiness, sacrifice, and drawing His people close. You might not understand every detail of a prophet's message, but you might catch how patient God is with His people—and how heartbreaking their wandering is to Him.

You don't have to force deep insights out of every line.
You just keep showing up, trusting that God can use all of His Word over time.

Giving Yourself Grace in the Process

Growing through study doesn't mean you'll never:

- miss a day (or many days),

- feel distracted,

- wrestle with doubts,

- or forget what you read.

It means that, over time, you keep coming back.

You come back after busy days.
You come back after dry weeks.
You come back with your questions, your joys, your tears, and your uncertainties.

God is not tracking your reading like a scorecard. He's walking with you.

As you think about your journey with Scripture so far, you might ask:

- Where do I see signs—small or large—that God's Word has been changing me?

- Are there ways I react differently now than I did years ago?

- How might God be encouraging me to keep going, even if I don't always "feel" the growth?

You don't have to have impressive answers.
Even the awareness that you *want* to grow is itself a sign that God is at work.

A Quiet Confidence

At the end of the day, growing through study is less about us proving our devotion and more about us trusting God's faithfulness.

He has promised that His Word is living and active.
He has promised that it will not return to Him empty, but will accomplish what He intends.
He has promised to use it to teach, correct, and train us.

Your part is to show up with an open heart.
His part is to do the deep work only He can do.

As we move into the next part of this book, we'll begin to look at how knowledge, understanding, and wisdom show up in different areas of life—relationships, decisions, trials, and more. But remember this as we leave Part III:

Every time you open God's Word, you are placing yourself in a position to grow—even if you don't feel it right away.

And little by little, often quietly, He is making you more like Him.

Part III

Living in Wisdom Every Day

Books by Rene'

Living in Wisdom Every Day

By now, we've walked through what it means to grow in knowledge, to gain understanding, and to walk in wisdom—and we've talked about how Scripture and the LORD shape that journey.

Part III brings all of that right down into the everyday spaces where we actually live: our relationships, our work and decisions, our trials and struggles, and the overall shape of a life that's learning to walk with God.

Wisdom is not just an idea for Bible studies and church services.
It shows up in the way we talk to people, the choices we make, and the way we respond when life isn't easy.

You might notice that the situations where you most need wisdom often don't come with a warning label. They slip into regular days:

- a tense conversation that catches you off guard,

- a decision you didn't expect to make so soon,

- a disappointment that shakes you more than you thought it would.

In those moments, all that you're learning—about who God is, what His Word says, and how He's led you in the past—can come together to guide you. Not perfectly, not without mistakes, but with a growing steadiness.

In this part of the book, we'll explore three big areas:

- **Wisdom in Relationships** – how God's heart shapes the way we love, listen, forgive, and speak.

- **Wisdom in Work and Decisions** – how we invite God into our choices, efforts, and callings.

- **Wisdom in Trials and Faith** – how we walk with God when life is hard, confusing, or painful.

You'll notice the same conversational tone and gentle questions you've seen throughout this book. The goal is not to give a list of rules, but to walk alongside you as you think about how wisdom might already be at work in your life—and where God may be inviting you to grow.

Let's begin where much of our daily joy and pain is felt: our relationships.

Chapter 9

Wisdom in Relationships

If there is any area where we feel our need for wisdom every single day, it's in our relationships.

Family. Friends. Church. Co-workers. Neighbors.
Even strangers we brush past in stores or online.

We can know a lot of Bible, pray sincerely, and love God deeply—and still find ourselves saying the wrong thing, reacting too quickly, holding grudges, or shutting down when we feel misunderstood. Relationships bring out the best and the worst in us. They reveal where wisdom is growing...and where it's still under construction.

Have you ever walked away from a conversation thinking, *I wish I had handled that differently?*
Or maybe you stayed quiet and later thought, *I should have spoken up.*

Those are the places where wisdom has something to say.

Wisdom and the Way We Speak

So much of relational wisdom shows up in our words.

The Bible has a lot to say about the tongue—how powerful it is, how it can bring life or damage, how important it is to be slow to speak and quick to listen. Sometimes we're tempted to think wisdom means having the perfect thing to say. But often, wisdom starts with *when not to speak*.

Have you noticed how easy it is to talk from reaction instead of reflection?
Someone says something sharp, and words rise up in you immediately—defensive, sarcastic, or cutting. In that split second, wisdom stands in the doorway and asks, *"Do you really want to say that?"*

Wisdom in relationships often sounds like:

- "Take a breath first."

- "Listen all the way through."

- "Ask a question instead of assuming."

- "You don't have to answer everything right now."

Can you remember a time when holding your tongue turned out better than "winning" the moment?
Those are traces of wisdom growing in how you speak.

Wisdom and Listening

Listening is one of the simplest, and yet hardest, ways to love people.

We live in a world where everyone is eager to be heard—and not nearly as eager to truly hear. Wisdom invites us to slow down enough to see the person in front of us, not just their words.

Sometimes, what someone says isn't the whole story. Underneath anger might be hurt. Underneath distance might be fear. Underneath harsh words might be deep disappointment.

If we rush to defend ourselves or fix the situation without listening, we may miss what's really going on.

Have you ever had someone really listen to you—not to argue, not to correct, but to understand?
How did that feel?

Wisdom in relationships asks, *"What might this person be carrying that I don't see?"* It doesn't excuse wrong behavior, but it acknowledges that people are more than their worst moment.

Wisdom, Love, and Boundaries

One of the tricky parts of relationships is knowing how to balance love and boundaries.

God calls us to be kind, forgiving, patient, and gracious. At the same time, wisdom recognizes that we are not called to allow ongoing harm, abuse, or manipulation. Loving someone does not mean letting them do whatever they want in our lives.

Wisdom might look like:

- Saying "no" when you're always saying "yes" out of fear.

- Creating space when patterns of behavior are unhealthy.

- Deciding not to continue certain conversations that always pull you into the same destructive place.

- Seeking help, counsel, or support when a situation is more than you can handle alone.

Have you ever felt guilty for even *thinking* about creating boundaries, as if it meant you didn't love someone enough?

Wisdom reminds us that even Jesus sometimes withdrew from crowds, confronted harmful behavior, and didn't entrust Himself to everyone.

Boundaries are not a lack of love.
Sometimes, they are love with clarity.

The Hard Work of Forgiveness

If there's one area where wisdom feels especially costly, it's forgiveness.

Forgiveness does not mean pretending something didn't hurt. It doesn't mean saying what happened was okay. It doesn't always mean trust is immediately restored or that the relationship goes back to what it was.

Forgiveness is releasing our right to hold the offense over someone, choosing to let God be the ultimate judge, and refusing to let bitterness be the final word.

That is not easy. It often takes time. Sometimes, it's a process of forgiving again when the memory comes back and the pain resurfaces.

Have you ever had God nudge you about someone you still hold in your heart with a tight fist—even if you smile at them on the outside?
Wisdom doesn't say, "Just get over it."
Wisdom says, "Bring this to God. Let Him help you release what you were never meant to carry alone."

There's a quiet strength in forgiveness—not weakness. It's choosing not to be chained to what someone else did or didn't do.

Owning Our Part

In any relationship, it's easy to see what the other person did wrong. Our own part is often harder to look at.

Wisdom in relationships includes the courage to say:

- "I was wrong."

- "I'm sorry."

- "I spoke too quickly."

- "I didn't listen to you."

- "Will you forgive me?"

Those words can be hard to get out. Pride doesn't like them. Fear worries they'll be used against us. But wisdom knows that humility is a path to healing and deeper connection.

Have you seen how walls can start to come down when someone sincerely owns their part, without excuses?
Sometimes, the wisest thing we can do is be the first one to soften.

That doesn't mean everything is fixed instantly. But it opens a door that harshness can never open.

Trusting God with What You Can't Fix

One of the most humbling realities in relationships is that you can't control another person's heart.

You can apologize. You can set boundaries. You can forgive. You can pray. You can show up with love and honesty. But you cannot force someone to change, see, or respond the way you hope.

Wisdom learns, over time, to bring people to God in prayer instead of trying to manage them.

- "Lord, You see this person more clearly than I ever will."

- "You know their history, their fears, their wounds."

- "Show me my part, and help me release the rest to You."

Have you ever had to surrender a relationship—or the outcome of a hard conversation—to God because you couldn't make it turn out the way you wanted?
It's not easy. But there can be peace in saying, *"I will love, speak truth, and act wisely—but I will not carry what only God can carry."*

Letting Wisdom Grow Over Time

You may be reading this and thinking of relationships that are complicated, painful, or confusing. You might be remembering moments when you were anything but wise. You might even be thinking, *If only I had known then what I know now.*

That feeling is familiar to many of us.

But instead of using that to condemn yourself, you can see it as evidence that wisdom has grown—and that it's still growing.

God is patient with us in our relationships.
He walks with us through misunderstandings, conflicts, reconciliations, and even endings. He teaches us through our mistakes as well as our victories.

As you think about wisdom in your relationships right now, you might ask:

- Where do I sense God inviting me to listen more than I speak?

- Is there someone I need to forgive—not to excuse them, but to free my heart?

- Is there a boundary I need to prayerfully consider?

- Is there an apology I've been resisting, even though I know it's needed?

You don't have to answer all of that today.
You don't have to fix every relationship at once.

Wisdom grows as you walk with God, one interaction, one choice, one conversation at a time.

In the next chapter, we'll step into another area where wisdom is needed every day—our work and our decisions. How do we invite God into the places where we plan, labor, and choose? How does wisdom guide us there?

Let's go there together.

Chapter 10

Wisdom in Work and Decisions

Every day, whether we realize it or not, we are making decisions.

Some feel small: what to wear, what to cook, what to tackle first on the to-do list. Others feel heavier: how to handle a situation at work, whether to take on a new responsibility, how to respond to an opportunity, when to say yes—and when to say no.

Work and decisions are two places where wisdom quietly shapes the course of our lives.

They are also places where it's easy to act first and pray later.

Have you ever looked back on a choice and thought, *I wish I had paused and asked God about that?*
Or found yourself so busy "getting things done" that you realized you hadn't even considered whether God was guiding what you were doing?

You're not alone. Wisdom meets us right there.

God Cares About "Everyday" Work

Sometimes we treat God as if He is mainly concerned with the "spiritual" parts of our lives—church, Bible study, prayer—and less interested in the ordinary tasks that fill our days.

But Scripture shows us a different picture.

God cares about:

- how we handle responsibilities,

- how we treat people in our workplaces,

- how we use our gifts and skills,

- how we carry ourselves when no one is watching.

Your work—whether it's paid or unpaid, in an office or at home, creative or practical—is not separate from your walk with God. It is one of the main places where your faith is lived out.

Have you ever sensed God teaching you patience, humility, or perseverance through your work?
Even on the ordinary days, He's present there.

Wisdom in work begins by recognizing that God is not just over your Sunday—He's Lord over your Monday through Saturday too.

Doing "Small" Things With a Big Heart

Not every task feels meaningful.

There are emails to answer, floors to sweep, forms to fill out, errands to run, and repetitive chores that seem to come back as soon as you finish them. It can be tempting to think, *This doesn't matter. This is just busywork.*

But wisdom looks at "small" tasks differently.

When we offer our work—whatever it is—to God, it becomes a place to practice faithfulness, diligence, and service.

You might ask yourself:

- *Can I do this with a grateful heart, even if no one notices?*

- *Can I see this as a way to bless someone else, even if it seems routine?*

- *Can I honor God in the way I show up, even in tasks that feel unseen?*

Have you ever had someone do something small for you with such care that it meant more than they realized?
In the same way, your everyday work can be more meaningful than it appears.

Wisdom doesn't measure value only by visibility. It sees purpose where others only see chores.

Inviting God Into Our Decisions

When it comes to decisions—big or small—it's easy to lean on our own understanding. We weigh pros and cons, talk to people we trust, and follow what seems reasonable. Those are all good things. But wisdom adds another layer: it invites God into the process.

That might look like:

- Pausing before you commit: "Lord, is this for me in this season?"

- Asking for clarity: "Show me if there's something I'm not seeing."

- Being open to "wait," not just "yes" or "no."

Have you ever been about to say yes to something, and felt a gentle uneasiness you couldn't quite explain?
Or felt an unexpected peace about a step that seemed risky on paper?

Wisdom pays attention to those nudges and brings them back to God in prayer.

This doesn't mean every decision will feel dramatic or mystical. Many choices will still require simple, practical thinking. But even then, we can say, *"Lord, I want to honor You in this. Guide my thoughts."*

When Paths Look Good, But Aren't Yours

Not every good opportunity is a God opportunity for *you*.

You may see a door open that looks exciting—for someone. You may see others stepping into things that look meaningful, impressive, or fruitful. Wisdom reminds us that calling is personal. What's right for one person in this season may not be right for you in yours.

Have you ever said yes to something mainly because you didn't want to miss out, or because it looked good on the outside—even though something in you felt unsettled?

Wisdom asks:

- *Is this consistent with what God has been speaking to me?*

- *Do I have the capacity for this, or am I stretching beyond what God is actually calling me to carry?*

- *Am I chasing this from a place of peace, or from fear of falling behind?*

Sometimes wisdom says, "This is good, but it's not for you—not now." That can be hard to hear. But it also brings a strange relief.

You don't have to do everything to be faithful.
You just have to do what God is asking of *you*.

Learning From "Wrong Turns"

Not every decision will be perfect.

You will have moments where you step in a direction and later realize, *That wasn't quite right.* You may take on more than you can handle. You may stay in a situation longer than you should have. You may miss an opportunity you now wish you had taken.

Wisdom doesn't pretend those things didn't happen. It learns from them.

Instead of living in regret, you can ask:

- *Lord, what are You teaching me through this?*

- *What signs did I ignore that I should pay attention to next time?*

- *How can I move forward wisely from here?*

Have you ever walked through a "wrong turn" that, in hindsight, became a classroom of wisdom?

You might not have wanted the lesson, but God still used it to deepen your discernment.

Wisdom grows not just from getting it right, but from letting God redeem what we got wrong.

Rest and Overwork: Wisdom in Pace

Work and decisions are not only about *what* we do, but *how much* we do and *how* we carry it.

In a world that often glorifies busyness, it can feel "wise" to fill every hour, say yes to every opportunity, and push past our limits. But Scripture shows us a God who rests, who builds rhythms of work and Sabbath into creation itself.

Wisdom in this area might look like:

- Recognizing when you're living in constant exhaustion.

- Admitting that always being "on" is not sustainable or holy.

- Trusting that the world—and your responsibilities—do not fall apart if you slow down.

Have you ever felt guilty for resting, even when you were clearly tired? Wisdom invites you to see rest not as laziness, but as trust: trust that God is still God, even when you step back.

Sometimes, the wisest decision is to pause, breathe, and let your soul catch up with your schedule.

Asking Better Questions

When facing decisions, we often ask:

- *"Is this allowed?"*

- *"Is this a sin?"*

- *"Can I handle this?"*

Wisdom asks deeper questions:

- *"Does this draw me closer to God or pull me further away?"*

- *"Will this help me love others better?"*

- *"Is this aligned with who God is shaping me to be?"*

- *"If I keep walking in this direction, where will it likely lead?"*

Have you noticed that some decisions aren't about right vs. wrong, but wise vs. unwise?
Not everything that is "permissible" is beneficial for you in this season.

Wisdom looks beyond the moment and considers the direction.

A Heart That Stays Open

At the core, wisdom in work and decisions is less about having a perfect plan and more about having a heart that stays open to God.

You can bring your spreadsheets, your schedules, your goals, and your dreams to Him. You can talk with Him about your job, your business, your creative projects, your responsibilities. Nothing is too "ordinary" to bring into that conversation.

As you think about your current season, you might ask:

- Where in my work do I feel most in need of wisdom right now?

- Is there a decision on my heart that I've been carrying alone, instead of bringing openly to God?

- Am I saying yes or no from a place of peace—or from pressure, fear, or comparison?

You don't have to figure it all out today.
Wisdom grows as you keep walking with God decision by decision, day by day.

In the next chapter, we'll step into one more area where wisdom is deeply needed: the moments when life is hard, confusing, or painful. Wisdom in trials looks different than wisdom in success—but God is just as present there.

Let's go there next.

Chapter 11

Wisdom in Trials and Faith

There are seasons when life feels fairly steady, and then there are seasons when the ground seems to shift under your feet.

> A phone call changes everything.
> A relationship breaks.
> A job ends.
> A diagnosis comes.
> A long-standing prayer still seems unanswered.

In those moments, our questions grow louder:
Where are You, God? What are You doing? What am I supposed to learn from this?

Trials press on our hearts in ways that reveal what we really believe. They test not only our patience, but our faith, our hope, and our understanding of who God is. Wisdom in trials doesn't mean we enjoy pain or pretend everything is fine. It means we learn to see our difficulties through God's eyes, not just our own.

Have you ever looked back on a hard season and realized you were not the same person afterward?

That something in you had deepened, even if you would never have chosen that path?

That's where wisdom and suffering begin to meet.

When Scripture Talks About Trials

The Bible doesn't hide from the reality of suffering. It doesn't pretend that faithful people never struggle. Instead, it speaks honestly and also gives us a strange instruction:

> "Consider it pure joy, my brothers and sisters, whenever you face trials of many kinds, because you know that the testing of your faith produces perseverance.
> Let perseverance finish its work so that you may be mature and complete, not lacking anything. If any of you lacks wisdom, you should ask God, who gives generously to all without finding fault, and it will be given to you."
> —James 1:2–5 (NIV)

Those words can feel almost impossible when you're hurting. *Pure joy? Really?*

James is not saying we have to enjoy pain itself. He's saying there is something deeper going on in our trials—something God can use for our good, even if the situation itself is not good.

Trials test our faith. That testing produces perseverance. And as perseverance continues, it shapes us toward maturity.

Have you ever noticed that people who have walked with God through real hardship often carry a kind of quiet strength?
They may have tears, but they also have depth.

That depth does not come cheaply. It is often formed in the fire.

Suffering, Perseverance, Character, Hope

The apostle Paul says something similar:

> "...we also glory in our sufferings, because we know that suffering produces perseverance; perseverance, character; and character, hope.
> And hope does not put us to shame, because God's love has been poured out into our hearts through the Holy Spirit, who has been given to us."
> — Romans 5:3–5 (NIV)

Again, this is not a call to enjoy pain for its own sake. It's an invitation to see what God can produce *through* it.

- Suffering produces perseverance.

- Perseverance shapes character.

- Character makes room for real, steady hope.

Have you ever gone through something that forced you to keep going one step at a time, where quitting wasn't an option? And somewhere along the way, you realized that your capacity to endure had grown?

You might not have noticed it day by day, but the trial was building something in you—perseverance, character, and a deeper kind of hope.

Wisdom in trials begins when we allow ourselves to ask, even through tears:
"Lord, what are You forming in me through this?"
not as a way to dismiss the pain, but as a way to invite God into it.

Asking for Wisdom *In* the Trial

It's interesting that in James 1, the invitation to ask God for wisdom comes right in the middle of talking about trials.

"If any of you lacks wisdom, you should ask God..."

That tells us something important:
Trials aren't just times when we need relief; they are times when we especially need wisdom.

We might pray, "Lord, get me out of this," and sometimes He does. Other times, wisdom looks like, "Lord, walk me through this. Show me how to respond, how to think, what to hold on to, and what to let go of."

Have you ever been in a situation you couldn't change, but you noticed God changing *you* in the middle of it?

That's wisdom at work in the trial—not only asking, "Why is this happening?" but also, "How do You want me to walk with You through this?"

When God Feels Silent

One of the hardest parts of trials is when God feels quiet.

You pray, and it seems like nothing moves.
You read Scripture, and it feels flat.
You go to church, and everyone else seems blessed while you feel empty.

Those seasons can make you wonder if you've done something wrong, or if God has moved away.

The witness of Scripture, though, tells us that many faithful people walked through times when they couldn't feel God—Job, David, Elijah, even some of the psalm writers who cried out, "How long, O Lord?"

Silence does not mean absence.
Delay does not mean indifference.

Sometimes, wisdom in trials looks like clinging to what you *know* about God's character, even when you cannot feel it.

- You remember that He is faithful, even when your circumstances are shaking.

- You remember that He is good, even when things are not good.

- You remember that He is near to the brokenhearted, even when you feel alone.

Have you ever had to say, "Lord, I don't feel You right now, but I choose to trust what Your Word says about You"?
That choice is an act of wisdom and faith.

Letting Perseverance Finish Its Work

James doesn't just say that trials produce perseverance. He adds, "Let perseverance finish its work…"

That means there is a part we play.

We can resist the process—becoming bitter, hardened, or closed—or we can allow God to use the trial to deepen us. Perseverance doesn't mean pretending everything is fine. It means continuing to walk with God in honesty, even when the road is long.

Have you noticed that sometimes our first instinct in pain is to pull away—from people, from prayer, from God Himself?
Wisdom calls us to do the opposite: to bring our hurt *toward* God, not away from Him.

You can say:

- "Lord, this hurts."

- "I don't understand."

- "I'm tired."

- "Help me not to give up on You, even when I'm struggling."

Letting perseverance do its work is less about being strong and more about continuing to turn toward God, even when you feel weak.

The Classroom You Didn't Choose

Looking back, you may see seasons that felt like classrooms you never signed up for.

Maybe you learned:

- compassion, because you went through something you once thought you'd never face;

- dependence on God, because your own strength ran out;

- humility, because you discovered your limits;

- empathy, because now you recognize pain in others more quickly.

Would you have chosen those lessons in that way? Probably not. But can you see traces of God's hand, even there?

Wisdom doesn't try to tie everything up with a neat bow. There are sufferings we will never fully understand this side of eternity. But wisdom allows us to acknowledge both: *"This was deeply painful,"* and *"God met me, changed me, or held me in ways I can't deny."*

Have you ever had both of those sentences living in your heart at the same time?

Holding On to Hope

Trials can be heavy. We don't need to minimize that. But Scripture insists that, in Christ, our suffering is never the whole story.

Romans 5 reminds us that the path from suffering to perseverance, to character, to hope rests on this: "God's love has been poured out into our hearts through the Holy Spirit..."

Hope in trials is not optimism.
It's not denying reality.
It's a deep, sometimes quiet confidence that:

God has not abandoned you.

This season is not the end of your story.

There is a future—both in this life and beyond it—where God's goodness will be fully seen.

Have you ever met someone who has walked through more than you can imagine, and yet there is still a light in their eyes when they talk about God?
That is hope, forged in the fire.

A Few Gentle Questions

As you think about your own trials—past or present—you might pause and ask:

- Where do I see signs that God has grown perseverance or character in me through hard seasons?

- Is there a situation right now where I need to ask not only for relief, but also for wisdom?

- Am I letting perseverance finish its work, or am I tempted to give up on trusting God?

You don't have to have neat answers to these questions.
You don't have to feel strong.

Wisdom in trials is often simple and raw: one honest prayer, one step of trust, one day of not letting go of God, even when you have more questions than answers.

In the next chapter, we'll look at what a life shaped by this kind of wisdom begins to look like—not perfect, not polished, but steadily rooted in God.

The Fruits of a Wise Life

If you've stayed with this journey—from knowledge, to understanding, to wisdom; from Scripture, to study, to everyday life—you may be wondering:

What does all of this actually look like over time?
What kind of life begins to grow out of this?

A wise life rarely looks flashy. It doesn't always get attention. It may not be the loudest, the brightest, or the most celebrated. But it has a certain *weight* to it—a steadiness, a rootedness, a quiet light that others can feel even if they can't explain it.

You can't fake that.
It grows over years, one choice at a time.

Have you ever met someone and thought, *There's something different about the way they move through life?*
Not perfect—but grounded? That's a glimpse of the fruit of wisdom.

Peace That Isn't Easily Shaken

One of the first fruits of a wise life is a growing sense of inner peace.

This doesn't mean you never feel anxious, sad, or overwhelmed. It means that underneath those very real emotions, there is a deeper trust that God is still God, and you are still held.

Over time, as you've walked with God through Scripture, through decisions, and through trials, you begin to see a pattern: He has been faithful. Not always in the way you expected, and not always on your preferred timeline—but faithful.

That history with God becomes an anchor.

So when a new storm comes, you may still feel the wind, but you're not quite as easily blown away. You find yourself saying, sometimes through tears, *"Lord, I've seen You work before. I don't know how You'll move this time, but I know You're here."*

Have you noticed even a small shift in how you respond to trouble now, compared to years ago?
That growing stability is a fruit of wisdom taking root.

Softer Heart, Stronger Backbone

Wisdom does something interesting inside us: it softens us and strengthens us at the same time.

On one hand, a wise life tends to be gentler. You've seen your own weaknesses, made your own mistakes, and experienced God's mercy. That makes you slower to judge and quicker to extend grace.

You might find:

- You listen more before forming an opinion.

- You're less surprised when people are imperfect.

- You have more room in your heart for people's stories.

On the other hand, wisdom also strengthens your backbone. Because you know God's character more deeply, you're less willing to be swayed by every new idea, trend, or pressure. You're more anchored in what is true.

You might find:

- You're more comfortable saying, "No, that's not for me," even if others don't understand.

- You're less driven by the need for approval.

- You're more ready to stand for what is right, even quietly, even alone.

Have you noticed that as you've grown, some things that used to offend you now move you to compassion—and some things you used to shrug off now trouble your spirit?
That's wisdom shaping both your tenderness and your courage.

Simpler Priorities

A wise life often has simpler, clearer priorities.

The more you walk with God, the more you realize you can't do everything, be everything, or please everyone. You begin to ask different questions:

- *What really matters in light of eternity?*

- *Where is God actually asking me to invest my time, energy, and heart?*

- *What can I let go of, so I can hold more tightly to what matters most?*

You may find that over time:

- Relationships matter more than appearances.

- Faithfulness matters more than speed.

- Obedience matters more than applause.

Presence with God matters more than constant activity for God.

Have you felt a pull in your heart toward a simpler, more focused way of living—even if your schedule hasn't fully caught up yet?
That longing itself can be a fruit of wisdom growing in you.

Quiet Influence

People who live wisely often influence others without trying to.

They may never stand on a stage. Their names may never be widely known. But the people who cross their lives are changed by the way they live.

A wise life:

- offers calm in chaotic moments,

- speaks truth with love,

- shows consistency over time,

- becomes a "safe place" for others to be honest.

You might not see yourself that way, but think about it:

- Have people begun to come to you for prayer, for perspective, or simply for a listening ear?

- Have your stories of God's faithfulness encouraged someone who was struggling?

- Have your quiet choices—choosing forgiveness, choosing integrity, choosing kindness—made more of a difference than you realized?

Wisdom doesn't boast about its impact. It just lives, and lets God handle the fruit.

A Life That Points Beyond Itself

The most beautiful fruit of wisdom is this: over time, the focus shifts away from us and more toward God.

A wise life is not a life that says, *"Look how wise I am."*
It's a life that says, *"Let me tell you about the One who has been so patient, so faithful, and so good to me."*

You might find that your stories sound less like:

- "Here's what I figured out," and more like,

- "Here's how God met me. Here's what He showed me. Here's how He carried me."

The more you see His hand in your knowledge, your understanding, your wisdom, and even your rabbit holes, the more naturally your life points back to Him.

Have you found yourself talking more about what God has done than about what you have done?
That shift is a quiet mark of wisdom.

Still Learning, Still Growing

It's important to say this clearly: a wise life is *not* a finished life.

You will still:

- have questions you can't answer,

- make choices you wish you'd handled differently,

- have days when your emotions run ahead of your wisdom,

- need God's grace just as much as you ever did.

But as you look back, you'll see a pattern—not of perfection, but of God's ongoing work. You'll see how He has walked with you through your curiosity, your mistakes, your creativity, your study, your relationships, your work, and your trials.

You are, and always will be, a student in God's classroom.
There is no graduation day on this side of heaven.

And that's good news.

A Few Reflective Questions

As we come to the close of this part of the journey, you might take a quiet moment and ask yourself:

- Where do I see fruit—any fruit—of wisdom in my life right now?

- How has God used my experiences, even the hard ones, to deepen my faith and shape my responses?

- What kind of person do I hope to become as I keep walking with Him?

You don't need to have it all mapped out.
Wisdom grows one day, one prayer, one step at a time.

Still Following the Rabbit Holes

We began this book with coloring books and "YouTube University," with pencils and paper, with AI art and greeting cards, with mugs, t-shirts, and stock photos, with sermons and phrases that turned into more than 30 books.

We talked about how one little curiosity can lead you down a rabbit hole you never saw coming.

Now, at the end of this journey, we can see that God has been using those rabbit holes all along—not just to teach you skills, but to teach you *Himself*.

- He used creative curiosity to show you what it looks like to seek knowledge.

- He used connections and "aha" moments to grow your understanding.

- He used real‑life choices, joys, and trials to develop wisdom.

And He's not finished.

As you continue forward, more questions will come. More Scriptures will open up. More experiences will shape you. More grace will meet you along the way.

You don't have to rush.
You don't have to know everything.
You don't have to be perfect.

You simply keep walking—seeking knowledge of the Holy One, welcoming understanding as He gives it, and choosing, day by day, to live what you learn in His presence.

That's the fruit of a wise life:
not a life without mistakes, but a life that keeps returning to God, keeps listening, keeps learning, and keeps shining His light in the ordinary and the unexpected.

And in all of it, He walks with you.

Still Following the Rabbit Holes

When I look back, this journey didn't start with a plan to write about wisdom. It started with **me**, a simple **adult coloring book**, and a handful of pencils.

I wasn't trying to become an expert. I wasn't trying to map out spiritual formation. I was just looking for a quiet way to rest at the end of the day. Then my curiosity woke up. **"YouTube University"** opened a new world—better pencils, different papers, markers, wax and chalk, pastels and pens. One small question led to another. One rabbit hole led to the next.

From there, my path widened into **AI‑generated art**, note cards and greeting cards, coffee mugs and t‑shirts, stock images and design apps, and eventually more than thirty self‑published Christian books. I never saw all of that coming. I was just following the next small curiosity, the next open door, the next nudge.

Somewhere along the way, you started reading this book and stepping into *your* own reflections—your questions about **knowledge, understanding**, and **wisdom**, your experiences with Scripture, your memories of trials and choices and conversations.

As you've walked through these chapters, my story has simply been one example. The real question underneath it all is:

- **How has God been leading *you* down your own rabbit holes?**

- **Where have your hobbies, struggles, and quiet moments become places where He's been teaching you, too?**

- **What comes first—knowledge, understanding, or wisdom?**

This book has been one long, gentle walk through that question.

We've seen how **knowledge** gathers truth—especially from God's Word—so we can begin to know the LORD, not just facts about Him. We've seen how **understanding** connects those truths to our own lives, as the LORD shows us how Scripture and experience weave together.
We've seen how **wisdom** is what happens when what we know and what we see begin to shape how we actually live—in our relationships, our work, our decisions, and even our trials.

But more than anything, we've seen that all of this is **not** about mastering a system.
It's about walking with a Person.

The same God who met you in your coloring pages and creative rabbit holes is the God who meets you in:

- quiet mornings with an open Bible,

- everyday conversations that need grace,

- decisions that feel heavier than you can carry,

- and nights when trials keep you awake.

He is the One who gives **wisdom**, and from His mouth come **knowledge and understanding**.

You don't have to turn your life into a project to find Him.
You simply keep saying "yes" to the invitations He places in front of you.

Maybe, for you, that next invitation looks like:

- picking up your Bible again and asking, *"Lord, help me see You here,"*

- paying attention to a verse that won't leave your mind,

- listening a little longer in a difficult conversation,

- or whispering, *"I don't understand this season, but I want to walk through it with You."*

You don't need to know the whole plan.
You don't have to feel "wise enough" to begin.

If all you can say is, *"Lord, I want to know You more, understand You more, and walk with You more wisely,"* that is already a beautiful place to stand.

As you close this book, remember:

- **Knowledge** will keep growing as you keep coming to God's Word.

- **Understanding** will deepen as the LORD connects that Word to your real life.

- **Wisdom** will take shape, slowly and quietly, as you live out what you're learning in His presence.

And through every rabbit hole—creative, ordinary, joyful, or painful—God will still be there, inviting you a little closer.

You are not finished.
You are simply **still on the way**.

Keep following the questions He stirs in your heart.
Keep noticing the doors He opens.
Keep walking, one small step at a time, toward the One who has been walking with you all along.

That is where true wisdom lives—
not at the end of the journey, but in the hand you place in His,
again and again, every day.

About the author

I've spent over four decades watching and participating in the digital revolution. From my first encounters with computer programming in high school during the late 1970s to navigating today's complex cyber landscape, technology has been a constant companion in my journey. While serving in the U.S. Army during Desert Storm, I witnessed first-hand how rapidly technology could evolve and transform our capabilities.

Now, as I navigate my senior years, I find myself in a unique position – someone who understands both the tremendous potential and the growing challenges of our digital age. This book represents not just my knowledge, but our shared experience as we continue to adapt and learn in this ever-changing digital world.

Through her writing, Rene' aims to illuminate the positive aspects of life's journey, drawing from her varied experiences to create stories that resonate with readers of all backgrounds.

Readers can discover more about Rene's work at https://books-byrene.com